Love Notes by Harpreet M Dayal

Sanvaad Publishing House

ISBN 978-0-9950527-2-7

For and because of my husband, Deepak Dayal
To my advocate and sister, Hardish Matharu
To my editorial adviser and friend, Simon J Allain

To you,

I hope these love notes find their way
to the love in you.

Love Notes by Harpreet M Dayal

when grey skies
close around your mind
with no sign of escape,
no hope of solace,
there is nothing wrong
in resting your head against
the shoulder of someone
who will share
a little of their sunshine
and a little of their hope
that everything will be okay.

you will
transcend
pain, joy,
and all things
in between
to find yourself.

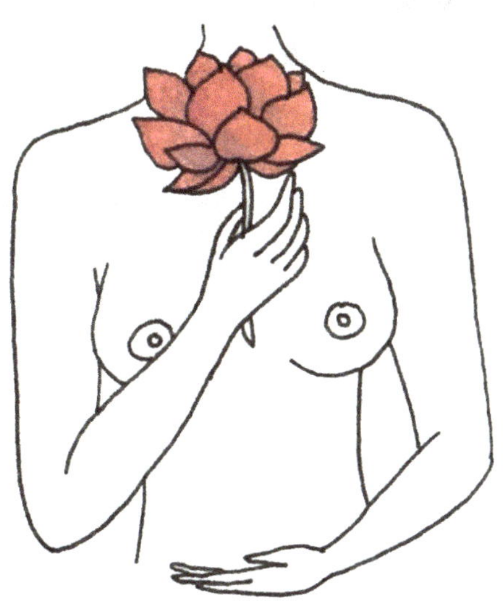

you are made
from the
bark of strength.

take a step back, my dear.
feel the soil between your toes.
plant, around your feet,
roses as white as the moon,
carnations as bright as the sun,
and sit in peace for a while.

at the end of it all
love calls out
from your every pore.

when worthlessness
sits under your skin
from words that
seep in like
poisoned rain
remember it will
sink into the marrow
of your bones
if you let it.

if you seek refuge
i've decorated a home
with your favourite things
inside my ribs.

honour every
ache in your soul
sit with every one
until they pass.

my dear,
the bud
must break
for the rose
to bloom.
it's okay to
break a little
to let them see
the rose in you.

there will be days when
you want to build a wall
around your heart.
but i say, be brave and
let in whatever life brings.
you were put on this earth
with the tools to
face whatever is coming.

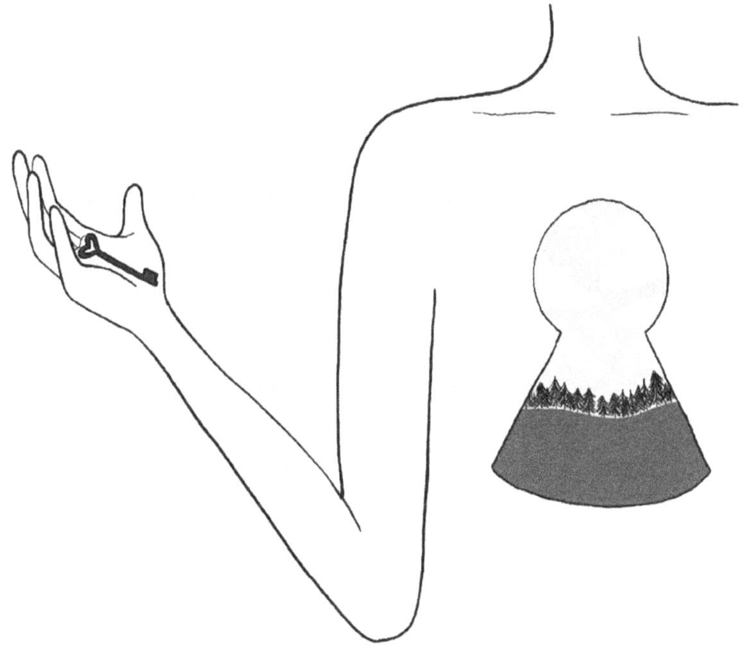

de-clutter
and let go
of all the things
from long ago
to make room
for love to reside
inside your heart.

when kindness arrives,
for a fleeting moment,
don't turn it away.
let it stay.

when you stretch your limbs
as the colours of the morning sun
stretch into the sky
tell it what you will create
with the day it has given you.

shed your bad days
with your tears.
the sun will soon
be here with sanguine rays
to dry them all away.

sow your home with love
and in time it will bloom.

when you follow
your thoughts into the
dark spaces of your mind
always go with a candle
lighting the way.

you must start from the inside out.
you have to water the buds of love.
only then will the fragrance
of their bloom drift to others.

worthiness.
it is there,
always there
and today
i hope
you find it.

it will never really leave
this love in you.

when you welcome
compassion with open arms
forgiveness will always come.

strength.
it will always
find you.
hold you.
console you and
lift you to your feet.

let what life has to offer
land in the softest terrain
within you
so you may always
come from a place of love.

lets not choose all the
reasons to break today
but all the reasons to mend.

love.
only love can
alter how we
see our own
reflection.

seeds of hope lay in the soil of night,
blooming into shooting stars
when the time is right.

melt into the night.
tell it stories of trials,
of all you have learnt,
and how after everything
you found your way home.

my universe, you are decorated with moons,
planets, brilliant stars, and the faith
that i have carefully placed in you.

when i stepped out of darkness,
my toes teasing the edge of the light
sunlight touched my feet,
the sun brushed my skin crimson,
warm wind embraced me,
and i placed flowers
at the feet of faith.

Harpreet M Dayal is an artist, learner and believer in the power of art to build connection, cultivate love, and heal. She is the founder of the Love Notes Project, author of children's book 'Wilbert the Worm,' and poetry book 'Svadhyaya: A Journey of Self Learning.'

www.ingramcontent.com/pod-product-compliance
Ingram Content Group UK Ltd.
Pitfield, Milton Keynes, MK11 3LW, UK
UKHW062254290726
14090UKWH00017B/686

9 780995 052727